Like This

poems by Susanna Lang

For information contact:

Unsolicited Press

Portland, Oregon

www.unsolicitedpress.com

orders@unsolicitedpress.com

619-354-8005

Front Cover Design: Kathryn Gerhardt

Editor: S.R. Stewart

ISBN: 978-1-956692-62-4

Table of Contents

Like This

We are like the clouds that pass and pass.
What does it matter then if we are not the same as clouds?
—Carolyn Forché, "Hue: From a Notebook"

We say *like* or *as* and the world is
a fish minted in silver and alloy....
—Eavan Boland, "House of Shadows. Home of Simile"

Like Apples

The young woman has forgotten the word for soul
in the language she heard on her first day in this world.

It is not a word for every day, not even over dinner
with her mother. Unspoken for weeks, it lies

buried under other words, other languages
that fill the streets of her new city.

Still, she once knew what it was.

Maybe she heard the word in a monk's blessing
or when she half listened to her uncle's stories

as she played among the rug's arabesques.
If she digs in the small garden that has been left to itself

behind their apartment building, dirt under her fingernails
and roots blocking her way, she might feel the word's edges,

the hard consonants, murmured vowels. She might remember
sunlight warming the mountainside near the village

where she first smelled apples ripening in the orchards.
That fragrance, apples in sun.

Like Bread

And snow crunches in the eyes, innocent, like clean bread.
—Osip Mandelstam

A year before he died
hungry and cold
in Stalin's work camp

Mandelstam wrote
about the miracle
of the breathing plain.

He saw the innocence
of the snow like bread.

Of course he dreamt
of what he didn't have—
but had the grace

to see beauty where
he'd been sent to molder

like bread left too long
on the kitchen table.
In exile he'd learned

to nourish himself
with sun falling across
the flat expanse of snow.

Like Coffee

I was driving home, not to the city where I live now, where I raised a child, but to the last home where I lived as a child with my parents. In the winter dark, the houses hunched into themselves, lights closer then farther away as the road wound through the hills, and I knew that at the end another house waited with yellow lights in the windows, door ready to open.

Mornings where I live now, the windows are still dark when I put water on for coffee. That house in my dream, or my memory, holds other stories now. My father no longer needs a house, my mother lives in the clouds. My city's streets run in straight lines, turn at right angles, though on late afternoon walks I can see into illuminated front rooms and almost read over the shoulder of the young woman sitting at her desk, head bent under the yellow lamp.

> Steam curls from the cup
> a scarf to pull tight against
> the leaky window.

Like Dogwood

The trees were tapers
lit in the woods
on green-gray mornings

when clouds settled
into the valleys

we didn't worry about fires then
or fungus rusting the leaves

I was a girl or a woman
depending on the time of day
and how far I could see

learning how to hold the road
on the curves

no streetlights or street signs
use your low lights in fog

If I went back now
following the roads

I'd be surprised to find dogwood
blooming in early spring

but I'd still find myself blinded
by fog—you can't douse fog
as sickness has doused the trees

Like evening

that arrives later each February day,
shreds of blue and brick
lingering in the air past five.

Like an echo that takes too long
to bounce back across a canyon.
My voice left unanswered.

Even the elephant god,
remover of obstacles,
can be delayed.

He knows how to wait,
his trunk in the honey pot,
monster mask behind his back.

Don't wish your life away,
my mother tells me.
The earth turns and the dark

will come earlier again.
Count how many minutes
you've gained today.

Like Franck's Sonata

That melody in the last movement: five notes, rising before they fall
and rise again a little faster, piano then violin and back
to the piano. *Allegretto poco mosso* but I did not know
Italian so I saw a mossy path through lilting hills, a slight breeze,
sun sweetening the air, enough time to walk the winding way home.
This when I couldn't walk at all, sick in bed my last year of college,
first apartment just off-campus, local station all I had to fill
the long hours when I couldn't open a book, day after day for weeks.

And then this melody I had never heard before, a pianist's child.
This melody singing that I would be well again, and soon if not
when the sonata landed at its triumphant close—maybe next week.
I would find that mossy path, marry my lover, learn Italian, move
far away, write better poems. No hills, but this morning the piano
climbs *allegretto* as if hills could be born again, all could be well.

Like goldeneyes

we winter here despite the cold when the golden-
eyed ducks fly further north.

This city, paved walks under the trees,
cast-iron fences:

this is the home we've made for ourselves.
The winter hasn't been harsh,

no blizzards, no arctic wind. Still, the river water
would slow our blood,

stop our breath. The ducks are serene
as they move together

in a swirl of black and white bodies,
a congregation,

a watery church, light sparkling on the surface
as if on glass

without stain, no reds or blues. No organ.
If they speak a little,

it is not in prayer. They would not know
what to ask for,

and if they praise, they praise each other's
gleaming eyes

and the river. Hosanna the cold,
the flowing water.

Like a Hawk or a Handsaw

I am but mad north-northwest. When the wind
is southerly, I know a hawk from a handsaw.
—Hamlet

Of course I can tell the difference,
can count the things of this world,
sort them into their separate boxes.

The handsaw in the toolbox
(though Hamlet likely meant a small heron,
a hernsaw as some called it)

and the hawk in my neighbor's henhouse,
the hens calling out to God and the poodle
and anyone else who could save them.

I know a button from a blowhard,
a pincushion from a pillowcase,
a needle in my mother's sewing kit

from the numskull who is setting landmines
for the rest of us to trip over
the rest of our lives. I can't sleep at night.

I can tell a siren that sings by the straits,
luring the sailors, from a siren
headed to the hospital,

whose call echoes in the still-dark room.
I know a rhyme that belongs in a bedtime song
    hush-a-bye
    don't you cry
from a reason that would be reassuring enough
to let me sleep until morning.

Like an Interruption

No signal.
Or an echo on the line,
someone else's conversation.

Except there is no line anymore,
at least not those iconic poles and wires
looping over the black-and-white prairie.

A man holds up his cell phone
to video the bodies in the back of a van.
Too many, he says. And disappears.

Warning bell, lights flash, the gate descends.
Nothing to do but wait.
One train, maybe two.

The Congress Hotel's lighted sign
has been nibbled at
by some electricity-eating creature.
Edited. Now it calls us to CONFESS
as we check in at the desk.

What have we done,
what have we neglected to do?

Like a Jot or a Tittle

tittle: a small mark in writing or printing, used as a
diacritic, punctuation, etc.

Like a note written in the middle of the night
or a pen stroke marking the absent letter.

Like a letter not delivered, or
a missing letter-writer.

Like a language spoken in five mountain villages
on the other side of the world, never written down,
seven hundred voices reciting the same words
so they remember.

What else is disappearing,
and how do we mark so many absences?

Here is a nest built last spring by a bird that will not return,
did we ever know its name?

Here is a stump, the ash tree cut down
after the ash borer devoured it.

Here the façade of a building hollowed by fire.
Where are the people who lived in these walls,
did we ever know their names?

Here there should be a gravestone
but in a time of plague we cannot hold funerals.
Will we remember where the dead lie?

Here is a mark, in their memory.
Here is another and another and another
in memory of all that has been lost.

A jot, a tittle, part of a word, a fragment of verse
in a language we are all beginning to forget.

Like the kingfisher

glimpsed, guessed at, flickering across the river and back, flash
of black and white, that upright spike of head feathers;

like traces of a fresco in the Kings' Chapel, upper body of a
woman in a white headdress, her hand on a stone tomb;
another's shoulder wrapped in a faded green shawl: all that
remains of grief;

like the ghost of a melody, heard once, that returns again and
again but only in phrases, never resolved;

like the woman of a certain age who dances at the water's
edge, bandanna over her hair, mask over mouth and nose,
light on her feet though she carries the weight of her years
around her hips;

like the round of dragonflies dancing over the woman's
head—they will soon be gone but now they keep time to
music they cannot hear;

like the kingdom of heaven, city on the hill, cloud cuckoo
land, all the shining places we imagine for ourselves in the
midst of darkness

Like Lemons

Francisco de Zurbarán, Still Life with Lemons, Oranges and a Rose, 1633

Lemons rest in the clean light of the 17th century,
their yellow reflected in a silver plate. Lemons,
a basket of oranges, a cup of water on another plate
with a single rose: three separate gifts,
the wicker neatly braided, the rose full open
and fragrant. We can pray to the Trinity
if we're given to prayer. The painter reveres the fruit,
the hands that polished silver, that wove the willow.

There must be a window above and to the left.
Dark wood, dark wall only a frame for the light—
they do not hint at grief or corruption, the fruit
unspotted, the rose unfaded. It is enough
to make me add lemons I do not need when I buy
beans to cook for dinner. I'll heap the yellow
in a porcelain bowl, white with a raised design
of chrysanthemums. Leave them to glow in the sun.

Like the mundane

details of daily life, hot bitter coffee with the morning paper,
a paper still made of paper that lands with a thump at the
        door,
crinkly with ink that rubs off on my fingers.

And along with the ink, the news that makes me reach
for the soap, that shuts the doors, that teaches the history.
We'd all forgotten the textbook chapter on Spanish flu

or only heard stories stripped to the bones, your father
who said he lived so long because he survived the flu
as a baby. We've turned away from the towns, the roads,

camps where it's not just the virus that kills all those who
        leave
in search of food, and those who nurse their hunger at home.
Where it's not a paper that lands with a thump at the door.

I wash my hands for twenty seconds and open my door
to walk the empty streets, Richmond to Wilson to Francisco
to Manor. I count the gardens where snowdrops are
        blooming,

I watch for purple crocus. At home I'll make more coffee and
    call
my mother who's dying of something slower, more certain
than virus. Another routine, I tend my mundane fears, my
    griefs.

Like the Narrator

If a story haunts me like the ghost of my great-grandmother
for whom I was named, may I tell that story
though it has nothing to do with where she came from
or the bed where I jumped to wake her each morning?

If a story speaks to me in the voice of my grandmother
who never told stories, who fled the pogroms
and shared my birthday, may I tell that story
though it is not related to me by blood?

> *It is like this,* begins the narrator, who might not be me.
> Our shelters are close together, the water comes in
> when it floods, the rats come in all the time.
> What do they bring us, the floods and the rats?

> I have heard that pennywort and garlic will ward off the
> virus.
> I have heard that prayer will ward off the virus
> and we answer the azaan, pray shoulder to shoulder.
> I have heard that all who fall sick will be killed, to ward
> off the virus.

The narrator has set the table with her great-grandmother's
silver,

she has fed the story her grandmother's kugel,
she has allowed the story to sleep at night in her bed.
The listener, who might be you, nods and sighs.

And this is where the story lives,
between the word breathed out and the word breathed in.

Like Onions

Now, everything makes me weep. Chopping onions, as always,
but also a cardinal singing from the bare branch outside my
        kitchen.

There is a woman in New York who buys yellow flowers
after her shift—if not daffodils, carnations, they must be
        yellow—
to place on the body bags stored inside refrigerated trailers
at the hospital morgue where she works. It makes me weep.

Before, it was Zogno and Bergamo where churches could not
        hold
all the caskets. Soldiers took them away, no one said where.
The priest rang the death knell once a day because he could
        not
ring the bell all day. He must have wept. In my neighborhood

there are few church bells and no balconies like those in
        Firenze
where a man opened his window to offer an aria to his
        neighbors
who sometimes hit the right note as they sang along, children
in their arms. The missing bells and the recorded arias make
        me weep.

But one of my neighbors plays a voluntary from the top of the
      kite hill,
sun glinting on his upraised horn. Near a shuttered bar

I find oyster shells washed up against the curb, and the city
      bus
stops to pick me up though I am only waiting to cross the
      street.

The bus driver's courtesy makes me weep.

Tonight I will make a ragù, starting with chopped onions
cooked in olive oil till they are soft and translucent.
They will fill the house with their fragrance and I'll weep again
because the onions will glisten in the pan like a memory.

Like Pliny the Elder

after the letter from Pliny the Younger to Tacitus,
translated by J. Firth

his body was found untouched

the air sulphurous, pumice-stones falling
they covered their heads with pillows

you ask me to send you an account
of my uncle's death

he had been curious about the cloud
rising from the mountain

all could see the sheets of flame

Rectina, the wife of Tascus wrote to say

(in the end he could come
no nearer than Stabiae)

she wrote to say that she and many others lived

the sea grew shallow, drawing back from the shore

he slept deeply, his servants could hear
his heavy breathing

pumice-stones and black flints
charred and cracked by the heat of the flames

others lived just below the mountain and could not leave
except by ship

                    his servants roused him
                    as buildings began to shake

              when daylight returned after two days
              the corpse suggested a person asleep

You will pick out what you think will answer your purpose
        best,
for to write a letter is a different thing from writing a history,
and to write to a friend is not like writing to all and sundry.

Like Quarantine

Except that we can still go to the grocery store, and yesterday we found fresh ginger for the first time in weeks.

Except that a man is measuring laps around the park for a 5K that may not take place, but he can hope.

Except that the song sparrows have returned to remind us more loudly than in other years *Put on the tea kettle-ettle-ettle!*

Except that we are not yet sick, and there are two of us inside these four walls.

Except that we cooked pork noodle soup with ginger, and agreed that one teaspoon of red pepper was enough.

Except that we played dominos and you won as you always do.

Except that we finally have enough time for you to clear winterkill and new weeds from your garden, and for me to write until I run out of words.

Except that there are voices shouting outside our windows, or sometimes just a man and a woman talking between themselves, thinking our house deaf as well as blind.

Except that our phones ring more often and I always assume it's bad news, your father or my mother or our son fallen ill but you are still there beside me in bed, my knees tucked into your knees, until I have to leave you there alone because I cannot sleep.

Like rain washed into the river

we are absorbed. Like a branch torn
from a tree on the riverbank, we rush downstream.

Like birds singing into the 2:00 a.m. dark
we are limited in what we can say
but required to speak. Like a bell rung only once a day
we call to others, we call to you.

It is a long way from where the river begins
to where it joins another, but unless rain becomes flood
we cannot change course. Nor arrive—
we are always on the way.

Like the river rising, we gather speed and force
as we go. Everything nourishes us.
We bear everything on our backs.

Like Snow in Early Spring

The curled leaves of the first tulips
hold snow like tasting spoons:
the calendar has been flipped
back a full month.

Though the snow melts by next day
we do not move forward, snowdrops
still blooming in every garden,
tulips not even in bud.

Still, at the end of the block
a mother and her small daughter
hang Easter eggs on fragile branches,
flecks of color in a monochrome print.

Like Talking to the Dead

They do not answer.

Freed from social distancing rules
they gather at the river,

catch up on news
from neighbors, parents, grandparents, children.

The boatman is delayed
but they are content to wait
in each other's company.

I imagine that river
like ours, brown and mucky,

whispering past dry grasses
drained of color.

Like the universe

expanding into what wasn't universe a moment ago, if
moments have any meaning for a universe.

Like our image of the universe shaped by the movies, all spirals
and sparkles on a bed of black with the inevitable speck
carrying our desires across its immensity.

Like the cramped interior of that speck, passengers contained
within smooth surfaces, buttons and levers under their hands,
the illusion of control.

Like the dreams of where those passengers came from, a creek
bordered by long grass where a child rode a pretend horse, or
the sound of voices raised, on a night turned unexpectedly
cold, to huzza a man who promised *We are, and always will be.*

Like the unicycle a boy rode to school each morning, a boy
who was named for the first man in the old stories, a boy who
kept his juggling balls in his locker and stepped on stilts to see
another world, a boy tallest as well as first, head nearest the
stars—

we whirl out through that blackness, that light, we reach
whatever unimaginable place we find after months, years,
centuries of imagining it; we walk through the dust or stone or
rushing rivers we discover there, and then we return.

We return.

Like Venus

Profound, the light on the nude Venus. So near, the
light whispers like the skin of a peach....
—Nohad Salameh, Baalbek

who sails bright-eyed
through the dusk
unfazed
by our streetlights, our desk
lamps

who lies in the
maple's arms
each branch
knitted to another's
buds

her hands, rustling,
riverine,
silky
like a peach ripening
in

a porcelain
bowl

Like a well

or the memory of a well.
A pump with worn

red paint
outside a one-room

schoolhouse
no longer in use.

Far north of here,
a hilly peninsula

that overlooks an inland sea.
I pulled the handle,

its joints complaining
loudly as my own

and wondered if
the well had run dry.

Only then the water—

slowly at first
then rushing

sweet and clear.
I had walked

a long way to drink
from this well.

Like Solving for X

We have not been careful
we have forgotten the steps

We know what the constant is
but have lost track of the variables

We have chosen the wrong operators
miscalculated the exponents
misidentified the expressions

We have not been careful in our count
we have forgotten the rules

Every number is now irrational
but we can verify that the numbers grow larger
even if mythical, the curve steeper

We have not been careful in counting the dead
we have forgotten the rules governing equations

The end point is vanishing
into the blank space outside the graph
and we will each solve for x
with our own logic
in our differential time

Like you,

like all of us,
I've had enough.

The days open and close on their hinges
like an old door that's shifted on its frame
and won't latch. Swings open
though no one touches the knob.

Like you,
like the door,
I'm tired.

It's been a long year after a long year
and it's not over.

You've seen more dark years:
born right before the Crash, of a father
who died young, and then war
after war after war for nearly a century.
Your heart is tired as the door, your legs give way,
your hands mistake the keys on the piano.

There are still days that sing.
Yesterday a flock of starlings talked it through
then lifted together into the sky
to weave their net around a red-tailed hawk

and force it down, feathers gleaming
copper in the slant of winter sun.

For me, that will do.
For now.

Even if you find a way to make that door close
and stay closed

I will be having this same conversation with you
for the rest of my life.

Like the Letter Z

The back-and-forth line of tracks through another snowfall
heavy on the daffodils, trace of some small creature whose
footprints I haven't seen before

The road that stopped unexpectedly at someone's barn—we'd
lost our way driving home after the eclipse

A cemetery no longer in use at the end of the dirt road where I
lived as a girl

The zigzag line climbing up the graph when up is the wrong
direction

The line of masked faces crisscrossing the parking lot outside a
grocery store

The final scene of a French movie from the '80s, a green ray
appearing over the water at sunset

The last letter in the name of the stone that glitters in the
creek bed, beneath a bridge where jasmine grows over the
railing

The last letter in the alphabet that holds all the words we
know, all those we've forgotten, and those we've never learned

An old man's last breath, alone in his bed at night

A card tucked away in a drawer, the last one the old man
signed

The last day of a fever, the last day we will be required to
remain in our homes, alone in our grief

> We are in the middle now
> but there will be an end
> or many endings

Acknowledgments

Grateful acknowledgment is made to the editors of the following publications where these poems or earlier versions first appeared:

Cimarron Review: "Like the mundane" (forthcoming)

The Comstock Review: "Like Franck's Sonata"

New World Writing: "Like an Interruption," "Like a Jot or a Tittle," "Like the Letter Z"

South 85: "Like Apples;" nominated for Best of the Net

"Like Quarantine" is included in *Art in the Time of Covid-19,* selected by the editors of American Writers Review.

"Like Solving for the Letter X" was short-listed for the Lockdown Prize by Fish Publishing and published on their website.

About the Author

Susanna Lang's e-chapbook, *Among Other Stones: Conversations with Yves Bonnefoy*, was released by Mudlark: An Electronic Journal of Poetry & Poetics in June 2021, and her translation of Baalbek by Nohad Salameh was published in October 2021 by Atelier du Grand Tétras. Her third full-length collection of poems, *Travel Notes from the River Styx*, was published in 2017 by Terrapin Books. Her poems and translations have appeared or are forthcoming from *Prairie Schooner, december magazine, Delos, New Poetry in Translation, American Life in Poetry* and *The Slowdown*. Her translations of poetry include *Words in Stone and The Origin of Language* by Yves Bonnefoy, and she is now working with Souad Labbize and Hélène Dorion on new translations.

About the Press

Unsolicited Press based out of Portland, Oregon and focuses on the works of the unsung and underrepresented. As a womxn-owned, all-volunteer small publisher that doesn't worry about profits as much as championing exceptional literature, we have the privilege of partnering with authors skirting the fringes of the lit world. We've worked with emerging and award-winning authors such as Shann Ray, Amy Shimshon-Santo, Brook Bhagat, Kris Amos, and John W. Bateman.

Learn more at unsolicitedpress.com. Find us on twitter and instagram.